Being Helpful

By Janine Amos and Annabel Spenceley
Consultant Rachael Underwood

CHERRYTREE BOOKS

A Cherrytree book

Designed and produced by
A S Publishing

First published 1997
by Cherrytree Press, a division of Evans Publishing Group
2A Portman Mansions
Chiltern St
London W1U 6NR

First softcover edition 1999

Reprinted 2000, 2001, 2002, 2003, 2004

Copyright © Evans Brothers Limited 1997

British Library Cataloguing in Publication Data
Amos, Janine
      Being Helpful. - (Growing Up)
      1. Helpful Behaviour - Juvenile literature
      1. Title
      302.1'4

      ISBN 1 84234 004 2

Printed in Malaysia

Joseph and Li

It's tidy-up time.

"Let's put everything back. Then we'll be able to find it tomorrow," says Dave.

Joseph puts the bricks back
in the box.

Li puts the dough in the tub.

Li finds a brick in the dough.
He takes it to Joseph.

Joseph has packed all the bricks
away.

Li is still busy.
What could Joseph do?

Joseph goes over to Li.
"I can help you now," he says.

They clear up the rest of the
dough together.

"We've finished!" says Joseph.

"You worked together," says
Dave. "You helped each other."

Harry and Rosie

"Waah!" Rosie is crying.

"She's been crying all night!" sighs Mum.

"Do you want your rattle, Rosie?"
asks mum.

"Nah!" says Rosie.

"Do you want your bottle, Rosie?"
asks Mum.

"Nah!" says Rosie.

"Brrr! Brrr!" goes the telephone.
"Waah!" cries Rosie.

"Oh, no!" sighs Mum.
How does Mum feel?

Harry goes over to Rosie.

He makes a funny face.

Rosie smiles.

Harry wiggles his fingers.

Rosie laughs.

Harry laughs too. "She's happy
now," says Harry.

"Thanks, Harry," smiles Mum.

"You helped Rosie – and that helped me."

Sometimes people need help.
Perhaps you can do something to
make things better.
Or you may need to ask how you
can help.

You might want help yourself
if you have a problem.
Who could you ask to help you?